Try Not

Would You Rather?

Easter Edition

Funny Scenarios, Wacky Choices
and Hilarious Situations
For Kids and Family

 RIDDLELAND

© Copyright 2020 by Riddleland - All rights reserved.
This declaration is deemed fair and valid by both the American Bar Association and the Committee of Publishers Association and is legally binding throughout the United States.

Furthermore, the transmission, duplication or reproduction of any of the following work including specific information will be considered an illegal act irrespective of if it is done electronically or in print. This extends to creating a secondary or tertiary copy of the work or a recorded copy and is only allowed with express written consent from the Publisher. All additional rights reserved.

Introduction

"The great gift of Easter is hope."
~ Basil Hume

We would like to personally thank you for purchasing this book. **Would you rather? Easter Edition** is a collection of the funniest scenarios, wacky choices, and hilarious situations for kids and adults to choose from.

These questions are an excellent way to get a conversation started in a fun and exciting way. Also, by asking "Why" after a "would you rather question", you may find interesting answers and learn a lot about a person.

We wrote this book because we want children to be encouraged to read more, think and grow. As parents, we know that when children play games and learn, they are being educated whilst having so much fun that they don't even realize they're learning and developing valuable life skills.

'Would you Rather …' is one of our favorite games to play as a family. Some of the 'would you rather …' scenarios have had us in fits of giggles, others have generated reactions such as: "eeeeeeuuugh that's gross!" and yet others still really make us think and reflect and consider our decisions.

Besides having fun, playing the game also has other benefits such as:

- **Communication** – This game helps children to interact, read aloud and listen to others. It's a great way to connect. It's a fun way for parents to get their children interacting with them, without a formal awkward conversation. The game can help to get to know someone better and learn about their likes, dislikes, and values.

- **Builds Confidence** – Children get used to pronouncing vocabulary, asking questions and it helps to deal with shyness.

- **Develops Critical Thinking** – It helps children to defend and justify the rationale for their choices and can generate discussions and debates. Parents playing this game with young children can give them prompting questions about their answers to help them reach logical and sensible decisions.

- **Improves Vocabulary** – Children will be introduced to new words in the questions, and the context of them will help them remember them because the game is fun.

- **Encourages Equality and Diversity** – Considering other people's answers, even if they differ from your own, is important for respect, equality, diversity, tolerance, acceptance, and inclusivity. Some questions may get children to think about options available to them, that don't fall into gendered stereotypes, i.e., careers or activities that challenge the norm.

Riddleland Bonus Play

Join our special Facebook Group at
Riddleland For Kids

or

send an email to:
Riddleland@riddlelandforkids.com
and you will get the following

- 💙 50 Bonus Jokes and Riddles
- 💙 An entry in our Monthly Giveaway of $25 Amazon Gift card!
- 💙 Early access to new books

We draw a new winner each month and will contact you via email or the Facebook group.

Good Luck!

The Try Not to Laugh Challenge
Would You Rather?

Easter Edition

How do you play?
The Would You Rather Challenge is made up of 10 rounds with 1 tie-breaker round at the end. At least 2 players are needed to play this game. Face your opponent and decide who is **Easter Bunny 1** and **Easter Bunny 2**. If you have 3 or 4 players, you can decide which player belongs to **Bunny Group 1** and **Bunny Group 2**. The goal of the game is to score points by making the other players laugh.

After completing each round, tally up the points and whoever gets the most points is the **Round Champion**. Add all the points from the 10 rounds to see who is **the Laugh Champion**. If there is a tie, go for the tie-breaker round where the winner takes all.

What are the rules?
Easter Bunny 1 starts first. **Easter Bunny 1** reads the questions aloud and chooses an answer. The same player will then explain why they chose the answer in the silliest and wackiest way possible. If the reason makes **Easter Bunny 2** laugh, then **Easter Bunny 1** scores a Funny point. Takes turns going back and forth, and write down the score at the end of each round.

How do you get started?
Flip a coin. The **Easter Bunny** that guess it correctly starts first.

BONUS TIP: Making funny voices, silly dance moves or wacky facial expression will make your opponent laugh!

Most Importantly: Remember to have fun and enjoy the game!

ROUND 1

 Easter Bunny 1

Don't Forget to Explain Your Answer

Would you rather be the Easter Bunny for one Easter OR help the Easter Bunny hide eggs every year?

Funny Point____/1

• • • • • • • • • • • • • • • •

Would you rather eat only chocolate for the rest of your life OR never eat chocolate again?

Funny Point____/1

🐰 Easter Bunny 1

Don't Forget to Explain Your Answer

Would you rather search for 100 chocolate eggs that are easy to find OR 1,000 chocolate eggs that are hard to find?

Funny Point____/1

Would you rather have a pet bunny that can talk to you OR a pet bunny that brings you chocolate eggs every day?

Funny Point____/1

 Easter Bunny 1

Don't Forget to Explain Your Answer

Would you rather hunt for Easter eggs in a huge garden OR in a mansion with lots of rooms?

Funny Point____/1

• • • • • • • • • • • • • •

Would you rather make a finger painting of a basket of eggs OR the Easter Bunny?

Funny Point____/1

STOP: Now pass the book to Easter Bunny 2

🐰 Easter Bunny 2

Don't Forget to Explain Your Answer

Would you rather be given a bunny for Easter OR a baby chicken for Easter?

Funny Point____/1

• • • • • • • • • • • • • • •

Would you rather have a lot of small chocolate bunnies OR have one 10-foot tall chocolate bunny?

Funny Point____/1

 Easter Bunny 2

Don't Forget to Explain Your Answer

Would you rather spend your whole Spring in the coolest treehouse in the world OR spend it at the best water park in the world?

Funny Point____/1

Would you rather have a garden where every flower is a different color OR where all the flowers are the same color?

Funny Point____/1

🐰 Easter Bunny 2

Don't Forget to Explain Your Answer

Would you rather get all the chocolate you want on Easter but none during the year OR get a piece of chocolate every day of the year, including Easter?

Funny Point____/1

• • • • • • • • • • • • • • • •

Would you rather have the Easter Bunny as a best friend OR the Tooth Fairy?

Funny Point____/1

🐰 Easter Bunny 1

_____/6
Round 1 Total Score

🐰 Easter Bunny 2

_____/6
Round 1 Total Score

ROUND 2

 Easter Bunny 1

Don't Forget to Explain Your Answer

Would you rather it rains while you're looking for Easter eggs OR it be nice and sunny?

Funny Point____/1

• • • • • • • • • • • • • • • •

Would you rather have an Easter egg hunt and find 50 eggs OR have 10 eggs be given to you straight away?

Funny Point____/1

🐰 Easter Bunny 1

Don't Forget to Explain Your Answer

Would you rather have to eat chocolate cake for breakfast every day OR eat chocolate pudding for breakfast every day?

Funny Point____/1

• • • • • • •• • • • • • • • •

Would you rather all of your candy taste like raisins OR all of your candy taste like nuts?

Funny Point____/1

 Easter Bunny 1

Don't Forget to Explain Your Answer

Would you rather search for 20 small eggs Easter morning OR eat 10 large eggs?

Funny Point____/1

Would you rather spend the whole Easter day with your friends OR spend it with your family?

Funny Point____/1

STOP: Now pass the book to Easter Bunny 2

 Easter Bunny 2

Don't Forget to Explain Your Answer

Would you rather have a big homemade Easter lunch OR go out to a restaurant for Easter?

Funny Point____/1

Would you rather go on a trip to Easter Island for Easter OR go anywhere else you want to go?

Funny Point____/1

🐰 Easter Bunny 2

Don't Forget to Explain Your Answer

Would you rather use a pirate map to find your eggs in a treasure chest OR use a riddle as a clue to where the eggs are hidden?

Funny Point____/1

• • • • • • • • • • • • • • •

Would you rather be able to use telepathy (read minds) OR X-ray vision (see-through things) to find your chocolate eggs?

Funny Point____/1

🐰 Easter Bunny 2

Don't Forget to Explain Your Answer

Would you rather let your friends help you find your eggs but you have to share half with them OR find your eggs all by yourself and not have to share?

Funny Point____/1

• • • • • • • • • • • • • • • •

Would you rather have the Easter Bunny be a giant, cool bunny OR a small, cute bunny?

Funny Point____/1

🐰 Easter Bunny 1

_____/6
Round 2 Total Score

🐰 Easter Bunny 2

_____/6
Round 2 Total Score

 Easter Bunny 1

Don't Forget to Explain Your Answer

Would you rather help your mom make cookies on Easter OR watch TV while eating your chocolate eggs and drinking milk?

Funny Point____/1

• • • • • • • • • • • • • • •

Would you rather be famous for singing a song about the Easter Bunny OR for writing a really cool book about the Easter Bunny?

Funny Point____/1

🐰 Easter Bunny 1

Don't Forget to Explain Your Answer

Would you rather dress up as the Easter Bunny OR dress up as a giant flower and go to school?

Funny Point____/1

• • • • • • • • • • • • • • • •

Would you rather have to eat a raw egg OR eat a cooked bug?

Funny Point____/1

 Easter Bunny 1

Don't Forget to Explain Your Answer

Would you rather eat a burger that is shaped like a bunny OR eat a pancake that tastes like chicken?

Funny Point____/1

Would you rather drink water that tastes like chocolate-flavored milk OR eat chocolate that tastes like water?

Funny Point____/1

STOP: Now pass the book to Easter Bunny 2

🐰 Easter Bunny 2

Don't Forget to Explain Your Answer

Would you rather have a fridge filled with chocolate eggs OR have a chocolate bunny the size of a fridge?

Funny Point____/1

Would you rather have a room filled with flowers that smell nice OR have a garden filled with flowers that smell bad?

Funny Point____/1

Easter Bunny 2

Don't Forget to Explain Your Answer

Would you rather have your hair a bright pink color OR have your hair look like a flower?

Funny Point____/1

• • • • • • • • • • • • • • • •

Would you rather have the Easter Bunny be your father OR have an Easter chicken as your brother?

Funny Point____/1

🐰 Easter Bunny 2

Don't Forget to Explain Your Answer

Would you rather have Easter be on the same day as your birthday and get twice as many eggs OR have Easter come twice a year but be several months apart?

Funny Point____/1

• • • • • • • ● ● • • • • • • • ●

Would you rather have ears and teeth like a bunny OR have a big fluffy tail like a bunny?

Funny Point____/1

🐰 Easter Bunny 1

_____/6
Round 3 Total Score

🐰 Easter Bunny 2

_____/6
Round 3 Total Score

ROUND 4

🐰 Easter Bunny 1

Don't Forget to Explain Your Answer

Would you rather have the first day of Spring be very hot OR be cloudy and wet?

Funny Point____/1

• • • • • • • • • • • • • • • •

Would you rather have a pet cat that poops out chocolate OR have a pet dog that is made of chocolate?

Funny Point____/1

🐰 Easter Bunny 1

Don't Forget to Explain Your Answer

Would you rather have flowers that can talk OR mushrooms that turn into fairies on the first day of Spring?

Funny Point____/1

Would you rather have spring vacation OR have summer vacation from school?

Funny Point____/1

🐰 Easter Bunny 1

Don't Forget to Explain Your Answer

Would you rather have an Easter egg hunt under the ocean OR on top of the world's highest mountain?

Funny Point____/1

• • • • • • • • • • • • • • • • •

Would you rather be able to hop really high like a kangaroo OR be able to hop really fast like a bunny?

Funny Point____/1

STOP: Now pass the book to Easter Bunny 2

🐰 Easter Bunny 2

Don't Forget to Explain Your Answer

Would you rather have to wear an Easter hat made of colorful flowers OR wear an Easter hat made of fake, colorful chocolate eggs?

Funny Point____/1

• • • • • • •• • • • • • • •

Would you rather have hot-cross buns with milk on Easter morning OR chocolate cookies and milk?

Funny Point____/1

Easter Bunny 2

Don't Forget to Explain Your Answer

Would you rather be able to turn into a butterfly whenever you want OR have a giant pet butterfly to fly on?

Funny Point____/1

Would you rather have the ability to make flowers grow really fast and big OR have the ability to make a wish every time you pick a flower?

Funny Point____/1

🐰 Easter Bunny 2

Don't Forget to Explain Your Answer

Would you rather have a baby lamb that helped you find your eggs OR a giant lamb that you can ride?

Funny Point____/1

• • • • • • • • • • • • • • • •

Would you rather wake up the next morning with bird wings but you can't fly OR with bunny feet that don't fit into any of your shoes?

Funny Point____/1

🐰 Easter Bunny 1

_____/6
Round 4 Total Score

🐰 Easter Bunny 2

_____/6
Round 4 Total Score

ROUND 5

🐰 Easter Bunny 1

Don't Forget to Explain Your Answer

Would you rather celebrate Easter all year long OR celebrate April Fool's day all year long?

Funny Point____/1

• • • • • • • • • • • • • • • • •

Would you rather live inside a house made entirely of chocolate that you can't eat OR a house made entirely of flowers that glow at night?

Funny Point____/1

 Easter Bunny 1

Don't Forget to Explain Your Answer

Would you rather be a chocolate maker with your own factory, like Willy Wonka OR live inside a chocolate factory and be a chocolate taster but you can't decide what kind chocolate gets made?

Funny Point____/1

• • • • • • • • • • • • • • • •

Would you rather have to eat only white chocolate OR have to eat only mint chocolate?

Funny Point____/1

 Easter Bunny 1

Don't Forget to Explain Your Answer

Would you rather turn into a bunny for a whole day once a week OR turn into a baby chick every night when you go to bed?

Funny Point____/1

• • • • • • • • • • • • • • •

Would you rather have a magic egg that grants you one wish every day, but you can only wish for small things and you have a lot of rules OR have a magic bunny that grants you only three wishes, but you can wish for anything you want except for more wishes?

Funny Point____/1

STOP: Now pass the book to Easter Bunny 2

🐰 Easter Bunny 2

Don't Forget to Explain Your Answer

Would you rather be in a music band called the Hip-Hop Bunnies OR be in a band called the Cool Eggs?

Funny Point____/1

Would you rather have to swim in a pool filled with chocolate eggs OR swim in a pool filled with jelly beans?

Funny Point____/1

🐰 Easter Bunny 2

Don't Forget to Explain Your Answer

Would you rather eat meat-flavored chocolate OR chocolate-flavored meat?

Funny Point____/1

Would you rather celebrate Easter weekend in a jungle OR in Antartica?

Funny Point____/1

🐰 Easter Bunny 2

Don't Forget to Explain Your Answer

Would you rather meet the Easter Bunny OR meet the Sandman?

Funny Point____/1

• • • • • • • • • • • • • • •

Would you rather travel to Easter Island on a magic flying carpet OR through an underground rabbit tunnel?

Funny Point____/1

🐰 Easter Bunny 1

_____/6
Round 5 Total Score

🐰 Easter Bunny 2

_____/6
Round 5 Total Score

ROUND 6

 Easter Bunny 1

Don't Forget to Explain Your Answer

Would you rather have to paint all of your Easter eggs with one color OR have to paint each one a different color and weird patterns?

Funny Point____/1

• • • • • • • • • • • • • • • •

Would you rather have to go to school on Easter day but get the rest of the month off or get only Easter day off and have to go to school for the rest of the month?

Funny Point____/1

 Easter Bunny 1

Don't Forget to Explain Your Answer

Would you rather go trick or treating for candy OR go egg hunting for Easter eggs?

Funny Point____/1

Would you rather all of your eggs be easy to find but they don't taste good OR all of your eggs be really hard to find but they taste like the best chocolate in the world?

Funny Point____/1

 Easter Bunny 1

Don't Forget to Explain Your Answer

Would you rather only be able to smell chocolate and nothing else OR be able to smell anything except chocolate?

Funny Point____/1

• • • • • • • • • • • • • • •

Would you rather have a giant bunny you can ride or a giant flying baby chick that you can ride?

Funny Point____/1

STOP: Now pass the book to Easter Bunny 2

Easter Bunny 2

Don't Forget to Explain Your Answer

Would you rather stay up late on the night before Easter and wake up late to search for eggs or go to bed early on the night before Easter and wake up early to search for eggs?

Funny Point____/1

• • • • • • • • • • • • • • •

Would you rather only be able to taste chocolate and not be able to taste anything else or be able to taste everything except chocolate?

Funny Point____/1

🐰 Easter Bunny 2

Don't Forget to Explain Your Answer

Would you rather have a best friend that helps you to find all of your eggs but then insists on you giving him half of them OR have a best friend that doesn't help you find your eggs at all and you don't need to share any with him?

Funny Point____/1

• • • • • • • • • • • • • • • •

Would you rather all of your Easter chocolate taste a little weird OR get no Easter chocolate at all?

Funny Point____/1

Easter Bunny 2

Don't Forget to Explain Your Answer

Would you rather have to eat all of your Easter chocolate on Easter OR only be able to eat one Easter chocolate a day until it's all finished?

Funny Point____/1

• • • • • • • • • • • • • • •

Would you rather be the star in a movie about Easter OR be the writer of a book about Easter?

Funny Point____/1

🐰 Easter Bunny 1

_____/6
Round 6 Total Score

🐰 Easter Bunny 2

_____/6
Round 6 Total Score

ROUND 7

 Easter Bunny 1

Don't Forget to Explain Your Answer

Would you rather be the Easter bunny in a school play OR be a big, singing egg in a school play?

Funny Point____/1

Would you rather only be able to eat spicy chocolate for the rest of your life OR never be able to eat any kind of chocolate again?

Funny Point____/1

🐰 Easter Bunny 1

Don't Forget to Explain Your Answer

Would you rather be able to visit the Easter bunny's secret egg factory and eat all of the chocolate you want while you're there OR be able to go wherever you want in the world?

Funny Point____/1

• • • • • • • • • • • • • • • •

Would you rather be able to taste every kind of chocolate that was ever made on Easter, but not your favorite chocolate OR be able to get your favorite chocolate on Easter, but now that is the only chocolate you can eat for the rest of your life?

Funny Point____/1

 Easter Bunny 1

Don't Forget to Explain Your Answer

Would you rather have bits of chocolate in everything you eat OR have jellybeans in everything you eat?

Funny Point____/1

● ● ● ● ● ● ● ● ● ● ● ● ● ● ● ●

Would you rather smell like flowers all the time OR smell like chocolate all the time?

Funny Point____/1

STOP: Now pass the book to Easter Bunny 2

 Easter Bunny 1

Don't Forget to Explain Your Answer

Would you rather have an Easter egg hunt on the surface of the moon OR have an Easter egg hunt in a giant castle?

Funny Point____/1

• • • • • • • •• • • • • • • •

Would you rather your father worked with the Easter bunny and brought home free chocolate every day OR you worked with the Easter bunny and not get free chocolate every day?

Funny Point____/1

STOP: Now pass the book to Easter Bunny 2

 Easter Bunny 2

Don't Forget to Explain Your Answer

Would you rather stay at home and search for eggs in your house OR go to your friend's house and search for eggs there?

Funny Point____/1

• • • • • • • • • • • • • • • •

Would you rather ask your dad to help you look for chocolate eggs OR ask your mom to help you?

Funny Point____/1

🐰 Easter Bunny 2

Don't Forget to Explain Your Answer

Would you rather have a brother that is really good at finding chocolate eggs and helps you or have a sister that hates eating chocolate, so she gives you all her eggs?

Funny Point____/1

• • • • • • • • • • • • • • • •

Would you rather be haunted by a ghost that only shows up on Easter and tries to steal your eggs OR be haunted by a ghost every day for the rest of your life, except Easter?

Funny Point____/1

🐰 Easter Bunny 1

_____/6
Round 7 Total Score

🐰 Easter Bunny 2

_____/6
Round 7 Total Score

ROUND 8

🐰 Easter Bunny 1

Don't Forget to Explain Your Answer

Would you rather have the Tooth Fairy leave money underneath your pillow when you lose a tooth OR have the Easter Bunny leave a chocolate egg underneath your pillow when you lose a tooth?

Funny Point____/1

Would you rather have flowers grow wherever you are OR have it rain wherever you are?

Funny Point____/1

 Easter Bunny 1

Don't Forget to Explain Your Answer

Would you rather find 100 of your favorite candy on Easter OR find one big present?

Funny Point____/1

Would you rather have it snow all day on Easter OR have it rain all day on Easter?

Funny Point____/1

 Easter Bunny 1

Don't Forget to Explain Your Answer

Would you rather bunnies could talk to you OR flowers could talk to you?

Funny Point____/1

• • • • • • • • • • • • • • • •

Would you rather be at a magic show and keep the bunny that the magician pulls out of the hat OR be the magician and be able to pull a bunny out of a hat?

Funny Point____/1

STOP: Now pass the book to Easter Bunny 2

Easter Bunny 2

Don't Forget to Explain Your Answer

Would you rather be the hare in the race and can hop very fast OR be the turtle in the race and be slow but win the race?

Funny Point____/1

Would you rather be able to control plants OR be able to control the rain?

Funny Point____/1

 Easter Bunny 2

Don't Forget to Explain Your Answer

Would you rather it snowed and was cold all year long OR it was Spring with lots of rain but no snow, cold, or hot weather all year long?

Funny Point____/1

Would you rather only be able to eat chocolate that is always way too sweet OR only be able to eat chocolate that isn't sweet at all?

Funny Point____/1

🐰 Easter Bunny 2

Don't Forget to Explain Your Answer

Would you rather be able to eat candies all year long but then there is no Easter OR only be able to eat the candies that you find on Easter and have no candies throughout the year?

Funny Point____/1

• • • • • • • • • • • • • • • •

Would you rather have to shower in chocolate milk OR have to bathe in caramel?

Funny Point____/1

🐰 Easter Bunny 1

_____/6
Round 8 Total Score

🐰 Easter Bunny 2

_____/6
Round 8 Total Score

ROUND 9

 Easter Bunny 1

Don't Forget to Explain Your Answer

Would you rather have a room filled with bunnies that poop chocolate eggs OR have one baby chick that lays golden eggs?

Funny Point____/1

• • • • • • • • • • • • • • •

Would you rather have to go trick or treating for your Easter eggs and have to search for candy in the garden on Halloween OR have the Easter bunny put your chocolate eggs underneath a tree and have Santa hide your presents in the garden?

Funny Point____/1

🐰 Easter Bunny 1

Don't Forget to Explain Your Answer

Would you rather the Easter Bunny hide the chocolate eggs at the end of a rainbow with a pot of gold OR the Easter Bunny bury the chocolate eggs in a treasure chest and draw an 'X' to mark the spot?

Funny Point____/1

Would you rather have Superman OR Batman help you look for your chocolate eggs?

Funny Point____/1

Easter Bunny 1

Don't Forget to Explain Your Answer

Would you rather swap Spring with winter and have a Spring that is twice as long but have no winter OR swap Spring with Summer and have a Spring that is twice as long but have no Summer?

Funny Point____/1

• • • • • • • • • • • • • • • •

Would you rather all your chocolate eggs be melted when you find them OR all your chocolate eggs be half eaten when you find them?

Funny Point____/1

STOP: Now pass the book to Easter Bunny 2

🐰 Easter Bunny 2

Don't Forget to Explain Your Answer

Would you rather do the Chicken Dance in front of everyone at school OR the Bunny Hop Dance in front of everyone at school?

Funny Point____/1

• • • • • • • • • • • • • • • • •

Would you rather have to carry one raw egg OR carry 50 plastic eggs with you wherever you go for a whole week?

Funny Point____/1

 Easter Bunny 2

Don't Forget to Explain Your Answer

Would you rather have a garden filled with fake grass that you don't have to water or mow OR have a garden filled with real grass that you have to water once a week and mow once a month?

Funny Point____/1

• • • • • • • • • • • • • • • •

Would you rather have a basket filled to the brim with small chocolate bunnies OR have a basket filled to the brim with chocolate covered raisins?

Funny Point____/1

🐰 Easter Bunny 2

Don't Forget to Explain Your Answer

Would you rather have flowers for hair or grass for eyebrows?

Funny Point____/1

• • • • • • • • • • • • • • • •

Would you rather turn into a flower OR turn into a plastic egg on Easter day?

Funny Point____/1

🐰 Easter Bunny 1

_____/6
Round 9 Total Score

🐰 Easter Bunny 2

_____/6
Round 9 Total Score

ROUND 10

Easter Bunny 1

Don't Forget to Explain Your Answer

Would you rather go out catching butterflies OR go out catching frogs on the first day of Spring?

Funny Point____/1

• • • • • • • • • • • • • • •

Would you rather be able to hop like a frog and smell like one OR hop like a bunny and have a white, fluffy tail?

Funny Point____/1

Easter Bunny 1

Don't Forget to Explain Your Answer

Would you rather have a lamb's legs OR have a marshmallow for a head?

Funny Point____/1

Would you rather carry a basket of eggs on your head for a week OR wear a really big, fancy hat for a week?

Funny Point____/1

🐰 Easter Bunny 1

Don't Forget to Explain Your Answer

Would you rather spend the first day of Spring chasing wild rabbits OR collecting honey from a beehive?

Funny Point____/1

• • • • • • • • • • • • • • • • •

Would you rather help your mom paint 100 Easter eggs OR help your dad paint two big trees so they look like Easter eggs?

Funny Point____/1

STOP: Now pass the book to Easter Bunny 2

 Easter Bunny 2

Don't Forget to Explain Your Answer

Would you rather eat grass that tastes like jelly beans OR eat mud that tastes like chocolate?

Funny Point____/1

• • • • • • • • • • • • • • •

Would you rather hide eggs for your friends to find OR search for eggs all by yourself?

Funny Point____/1

 Easter Bunny 2

Don't Forget to Explain Your Answer

Would you rather have a bunny hop race OR a duck waddle race?

Funny Point____/1

• • • • • • • • • • • • • • •

Would you rather go fly a kite with your family OR go swimming in a large pool with your friends on the first day of Spring?

Funny Point____/1

 Easter Bunny 2

Don't Forget to Explain Your Answer

Would you rather your skin change color when the sun comes out OR your hair change color when it is raining?

Funny Point____/1

• • • • • • ● ● ● ● • • • ●

Would you rather be only taller on the first day of Spring just like a flower OR grow nonstop all year round until you are 10 feet tall?

Funny Point____/1

🐰 Easter Bunny 1

_____/6
Round 10 Total Score

🐰 Easter Bunny 2

_____/6
Round 10 Total Score

Tie Breaker

Add up Each Player's Score From ALL Previous Rounds. If Points Result in A Tie, Move On to the Tie Breaker Round

Easter Bunny 1 _____/10
Grand Total

Easter Bunny 2 _____/10
Grand Total

 Easter Bunny 1

Don't Forget to Explain Your Answer

Would you rather spend the first day of Spring indoors OR spend the first day of Spring outdoors, even if the weather is really bad?

Funny Point____/1

• • • • • • • • • • • • • • • •

Would you rather have to wear really bright colored clothes OR only wear white clothes in Spring?

Funny Point____/1

 Easter Bunny 1

Don't Forget to Explain Your Answer

Would you rather have a large, plastic-egg-shaped body OR have plastic green grass for hair?

Funny Point____/1

• • • • • • • • • • • • • • •

Would you rather have to stay inside all day but it is really sunny and warm outside OR have to stay by the pool all day, but it is raining the whole time?

Funny Point____/1

 Easter Bunny 1

Don't Forget to Explain Your Answer

Would you rather dress up as a butterfly OR dress up as a baby chick on the first day of spring?

Funny Point____/1

• • • • • • • • • • • • • • •

Would you rather have ears like a rabbit OR feet like a baby chick?

Funny Point____/1

STOP: Now pass the book to Easter Bunny 2

🐰 Easter Bunny 2

Don't Forget to Explain Your Answer

Would you rather be part of the largest egg hunt in the world OR go treasure hunting with a real-life pirate?

Funny Point____/1

Would you rather play a game of duck, duck, goose but turn into a duck when you are caught OR play a game of hide and seek but turn into an egg when you are found?

Funny Point____/1

🐰 Easter Bunny 2

Don't Forget to Explain Your Answer

Would you rather roll down a hill of grass or swim in a pool of flowers?

Funny Point____/1

Would you rather wear a hat that is made of flowers, but it will rain over your head so the flowers get watered OR wear a hat that is made of chocolate, but if you stay in the sun for too long the chocolate will melt?

Funny Point____/1

🐰 Easter Bunny 2

Don't Forget to Explain Your Answer

Would you rather find a field filled with talking flowers OR find one big tree that can talk?

Funny Point____/1

Would you rather have a bunny hide your chocolate eggs OR have a squirrel hid the eggs the same way he would hide acorns?

Funny Point____/1

🐰 Easter Bunny 1

_____/6
Round 11 Total Score

🐰 Easter Bunny 2

_____/6
Round 11 Total Score

_____

**The Ultimate
Try Not to Laugh Challenge
Master**

Did you enjoy the book?

If you did, we are ecstatic. If not, please write your complaint to us and we will make sure to fix it.

If you're feeling generous, there is something important that you can help me with – tell other people that you enjoyed the book.

Ask a grownup to write about it on Amazon. When the do, more people will find out about the book. It also lets Amazon know that we are making kids around the world laugh. Even a few words and ratings would go a long way.

If you have any ideas or jokes that you think are super funny, please let us know. We would love to hear from you. Our email address is - **riddleland@riddlelandforkids.com**

Other Fun Children Books for The Kids!

Riddles Series

FUN RIDDLES AND TRICK QUESTIONS FOR KIDS AND FAMILY!
300 RIDDLES AND BRAIN TEASERS THAT KIDS AND FAMILY WILL ENJOY
RIDDLELAND

CREATIVE RIDDLES AND TRICK QUESTIONS FOR KIDS AND FAMILY!
300 RIDDLES AND BRAIN TEASERS THAT KIDS AND FAMILY WILL ENJOY
RIDDLELAND

FUN HALLOWEEN RIDDLES AND TRICK QUESTIONS FOR KIDS AND FAMILY!
TRICK-OR-TREAT EDITION: 300 RIDDLES AND BRAIN TEASERS THAT KIDS AND FAMILY WILL ENJOY
RIDDLELAND

FUN THANKSGIVING RIDDLES AND TRICK QUESTIONS FOR KIDS AND FAMILY!
TURKEY STUFFING EDITION: RIDDLES AND BRAIN TEASERS THAT KIDS AND FAMILY WILL ENJOY
RIDDLELAND

FUN CHRISTMAS RIDDLES AND TRICK QUESTIONS FOR KIDS AND FAMILY!
STOCKING STUFFER EDITION: 300 RIDDLES AND BRAIN TEASERS THAT KIDS AND FAMILY WILL ENJOY
RIDDLELAND

Encourage your kids to think outside of the box with these Fun and Creative Riddles!

Get them on Amazon

Try Not to Laugh Challenge Series

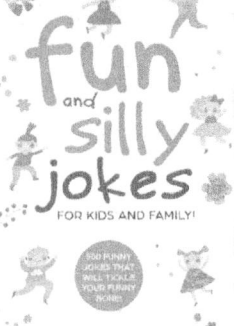

Get them on Amazon
or our website at
www.riddlelandforkids.com

Would You Rather Series

Riddleland Bonus Play

Join our special Facebook Group at
Riddleland For Kids

or

send an email to:
Riddleland@riddlelandforkids.com
and you will get the following

- 💗 50 Bonus Jokes and Riddles
- 💗 An entry in our Monthly Giveaway of $25 Amazon Gift card!
- 💗 Early Access to new books

We draw a new winner each month and will contact you via email or the facebook group.

 **Good Luck!**

RIDDLE AND JOKE CONTESTS!!

Riddleland is having **2 contests** to see who are the smartest or funniest boys and girls in the world:

   1) Creative and Challenging Riddles
   2) Tickle Your Funny Bone Contest

Parents, please email us your child's "Original" Riddle or Joke **and he or she could win a new Riddleland Book. Here are the rules:**

  1) It must be challenging for the riddles and funny for the jokes!

  2) It must be 100% original and not something from the Internet! It is easy to find out!

  3) You can submit both jokes and riddles as they are 2 separate contests.

  4) No help from the parents unless they are as funny as you.

  5) Winners will be announced via email.

  6) Email us at **Riddleland@riddlelandforkids.com**

About Riddleland

Riddleland is a mom + dad run publishing company. We are passionate about creating fun and innovative books to help children develop their reading skills and fall in love with reading. If you have suggestions for us or want to work with us, shoot us an email at **riddleland@riddlelandforkids.com**

Our favorite family quote

"Creativity is an area in which younger people have a tremendous advantage since they have an endearing habit of always questioning past wisdom and authority." - Bill Hewlett

Made in the USA
Coppell, TX
01 April 2020